PRAISE FOR MARK ~~~~~~~~~~~~~~~~
"CROW'S FOOT"

This book is a delight - poignant, deep, funny and evocative.
Mark Herzberger's dry sense of humour and keen
appreciation for irony sneak up on you with heart-piercing
truths . . . You feel like you're hanging out with a good friend
—one who continually surprises, enchants and sometimes
perplexes with the scope of his insight into human nature and
sympathy for our collective condition.
**~ Carol Casey, poet, two-time Pushcart nominee and
winner of the Stratford 2016 Open Mike Contest;
author of *What Can Happen: family and other
raptures of imperfection***

With vivid imagery throughout, Hertzberger's poems convey
an obvious love of words creating a truly cathartic reading
experience. Although each poem feels deeply personal to the
author, the universally appealing themes evoke a sense of
nostalgia that draws the reader in by tapping into something
innately familiar. . . .Crow's Foot is a thought-provoking,
exploratory dive into the past as well as a poignant look at the
present.
**- Michael E. Smidts, author, *One Hundred Words: A
Collection of Short Stories***

CROW'S FOOT

CROW'S FOOT

MARK HERTZBERGER

Storeylines Press

Land Acknowledgment

Storeylines Press operates on the lands of the Anishinabek, Haudenosauneega Confederacy, and Anishinaabe, Treaty 29, 1827. As settlers to this area, we acknowledge the rights and importance of the Indigenous people and their importance to this region, nation, and its culture, as well as their unjust treatment by the Canadian government and settlers past and present. We support justice for all missing and murdered women and girls, and healing for those affected by the horrors of residential schools and current injustices.

DEDICATION

For my mother, Bernice, who taught me that entire worlds can exist between the covers of a book

CONTENTS

Turn left at the crowsfoot,
every local knows what you mean:
as the crow flies,
to the crow's eye,
a giant avian footprint
from unknown roots;
originally indigenous or
imposed surveyors' boundaries?

Or simply the knitting together
of topography,
township roads,
and trailblazing
over arrowheads,
rusted ploughshares,
and the graves of field mice.

Like the lines that
crease the corners
of your tired eyes,
knitting together
sadness,
anger,
and laughter
where all can see
what was
and ever will be,
where you have been
and where you are going.

CROW'S FOOT

BETWEEN

When I sat small in my parents' house,
the stolid armchair stood
miles from the eternal couch,
a morning's journey by matchbox car,
delightful mishaps along the way.

When my bedroom window overlooked open
    fields,
my thoughts meandered
to the other side,
through the dark woods, past
watchful, shadowed burrows,
to the river beyond,
to the singing frogs.

Today, your music knits
my silence into patterns,
weds gently with my soul.
I run up the cloudy steps
to taste the view
from top of mood,
from summit of mind.

When I ask you for space,
if I ask for room,
it is for clarity not cloister,
sky not monastery;
the distance between us
I can skip in a heartbeat.

SEVERE WEATHER WARNING WITH 20% CHANCE OF FLOWERS

Kick to the back of my theatre seat
kick starts the amygdala;
cut off in traffic
cuts to the quick,
hurts in disproportion,
directly proportionate
to last night's slight;
where did it start and how will it end?

Limbic in limbo,
these days of dissolution;
spin our wheels and pray
for redemptive media;
spin and sink deeper.

Crack a smile,
break the ice;
take a step back,
step up to the plate;
take a breath,
mouth to mouth for humanity;

coastal winds almost within reach:
serene weather warming
with a 40% chance of peace.

WINTER SOLACE

Afternoon

In Walmart
plastic blooms
red and green,
bubble wrapped dreams,
cheap and brittle,
flank the aisles.

Shoppers weave,
dart,
bump,
eyes fixed and tired.

Herald angels sing from
ceiling tiles -
warbles and trills,
hymnal mutations,
familiar yet discomforting.

Outside,
black pickup
backs into black suv,
horn blasts exchanged,
paint and salt exchanged;
slush like dirty porridge
flung against my coat.

Evening

On the back roads home
pull onto the shoulder,
pull on hat and gloves,
wade knee deep through the snow,
stand dead centre
in the dead field,
let the cold suffuse my flesh
like whiskey down my throat.

Blue grey snow clouds,
farmhouse by a stand of spruce
across the drifted shadow sea,
buttery light from windows,
white plumes from a chimney.

Silent night

A forgotten feeling
blossoms behind my eyes,
holds my face
between its warm hands,
and is gone.

SINS OF THE FATHERS

His grandfather once bragged:
I can make any man cry.

He feels the weight
of ancestral baggage,
jacob marley chains
forged link by link,
blow by blow
over a century,
dragged behind him
erasing his footprints
as snow falls heavily.

His Lady Franklin,
searches for him,
shackled to a sledge
with her children;
shouts for him
across a blank canvas,
blurred indentations and ripples
her only markers;

She screams at his mirages,
drowns each time
in the deep silence,
the arctic's breath upon her neck.

TAKE IT ALL OFF

This beauty contest
is far too superficial;
so leave your tiara at the door;
take off your dancing shoes,
your silk stockings.

Now your necklace,
earrings,
rings,
bracelet.

Next the gown,
the lingerie;
don't worry,
we promise not to look.

Please don't stop there;
you can drape your skin,
tattoos, makeup and all,
over that chair and
fold your skeleton up,
put it in the closet over there.

Now, get ready to step onto the stage;
the contest begins.

Such a diverse display of contenders:
sullen shadows
brittle souls,
jagged dispositions,
dark silhouettes so thin,
so strangled by themselves,
they disappear in profile.

But there are others too,
their lights dimmed
by care and worry,
or needlessly hooded in shame;
still, they line up stage left,
hoping to shine.

So please, ladies and gentlemen,
applaud;
applaud with all your love;
show the judges who should win.

IN FROM THE COLD

Sometimes hear I them late at night
inside the wall next door,
squeal and thud,
chirp and snarl;
I wonder what they are.

My parents never listen,
my mom says not to lie
but I just can't stop hearing them
even though I try.

Hoots and screams,
they're not just dreams,
they really sound quite furious,
but they're not free
and I'm not scared,
just really kind of curious.

Saturday
the wall comes down,
my dad and uncle say,
to make room for the wine rack.
I try to warn amid their scorn,

but there's no turning back.

It's not for me to worry though;
I won't cry or pout; just sit with
a coke and a chocolate bar,
and watch what slithers out.

This house has many secrets;
it's time they all got told,
but if I just wait, it's not too late;
they'll come in from the cold.

GALLERY MILITARIA

Their portraits ensure places
forever
on museum walls,
these architects of death,
some impassive, some earnest,
others staunch, proud,
pompous.

Many preside over battle scenes,
yet are somehow
detached
from the fighting and muddy gore,
spotlit
in impossibly heroic contortions.

I have no quarrel with
honouring the dead
but propose an expansion
to include portraits
of all souls now tangled together
in the tactical reaper's suffocating robes:

On the wall under each officer,
the young soldiers
who perished under his command;

under each soldier,
the people he placed under fire,
friendly or unfriendly;

under each martyred soldier,
friend or foe,
the worn faces of his widow,
children,
parents
robbed,
beaten down
by fate and politics.

Finally, for the children never born,
the dreams never lived:
a family tree of
framed blank canvases.

JUNE 8TH

My bike leans against the porch;
the sprockets of my mind are still.
I sit on warm veranda steps.

A breeze nuzzles my shirt;
waves of gentle applause
ripple through
old maples' young leaves.

No fences,
no property lines
split my simple moment of
spring drift.

The calendar is mute and buried;
there is only time expanded,
the quiet emptiness of Sunday afternoon.

ANVIL

For my grandfather Eldon (1885 - 1938)

1909

In his own mind
he works in an egg,
a womb of darkness
lit by a fiery yoke.

Tongs and iron,
sledge and anvil,
the bellows
conjure constellations
against the shop's night rafters.

In his own hands,
the iron yields
like red taffy;
he is an aproned midwife,
coaxing steel creation
from a cauldron.

At noon,
in his own right
sitting under the beech tree,
feeling the tide in his muscles
ebbing,
the cool water
coursing
down his throat,
straight to his belly;
savours each bite,
cold pork,
cheese, pickle
bread baked by his young wife.

Immersed
in the blue and green
beyond the shell,
he thanks God
for the gift of contrast.

1913

Before he blacks out,
he glimpses the factory floor
fathoms below,
sees scurrying shadows
like rats:
his fellow workers

scrambling
to bring him
down,
excise him from the pulley,
his right arm now enmeshed
with the industrial age,
his soul in limbo
beyond the egg.

IN THE SHED

I read somewhere I can expect my skin to
     replace itself
every month, well
not exactly every month but really
how many of us keep track?

Certain snakes, on the other hand,
only shed their skin once a year.
His old skin gets dull and boring,
his eyes turn foggy,
he rubs his nose against a tree
to start things moving and
comes out the other end with
a stylish new suit
and freshly lasered eyes.

This doesn't work for me
even though I've tried
banging my head
against the wall in my office
numerous times.
My new skin looks worse than my old skin;
I still have scales over both eyes.

DAWN OF HUMANITY

He brushes whispers of winter
gently from our faces,
grey strands of cocoon,
old age made new again.

Freshly woken yet
dreaming still,
we stand naked,
poised
on the precipice of spring,
a sea of stars at our feet.

Each ovum of light floats,
bathed in the future,
cradled in Beauty
as new,
as Ancient
as love itself.

Wings unfolded,
we crouch,
lean forward
and push the Earth away.

HOW QUIET IT IS

After the snowfall,
how quiet is it?

So quiet,
if you think a secret,
the tree nearest you
whispers it to the next tree,
who whispers it to the next.

So quiet,
when the wind
hears your secret,
snatches it up
and floats it down,
you can hear it crying
outside your front gate,
miles away.

HOW QUIET IT IS . . . PART 2

After the snowfall,
how quiet is it?

So quiet,
that at the first sputter
of your neighbour's snow blower,
the drifted yard
like a bowl of cake batter
folds it and him
underneath
to join the land of lost toys.

NEVER LOOK BACK

Our house grew in a cornfield
from a tiny kernel
of artifact in emptiness,
rooting hard
against wind and sunsets,
anchored
by my parents' compulsions.

On the walls of my room,
shadows of imagined trees
bearing competing futures,
some boughs pendulous,
others dry and cracked.

In that room, I forged reality,
hammered its thin metal
into maps and timetables,
then stepped out,
never looked back,
never looked around.

I knocked against shoulders,
and felt the crowd separate.

Today,
I walk by my childhood home.
It hunches under entangled trees,
shabby, shamed and stuck,
abandoned
by a careless landlord.

I would never venture inside again.
It worries me to think
I may never have left.

CHRISTMAS WRAITHS

The ancient Celts believed that the veil between the world of the living and the world of the dead was thinnest during Yuletide. Later, in Victorian times, a passion for spiritualism led to ghost stories appearing in the many Christmas Annuals of the day.

As my disinterred family sits
chattering among themselves,
regret sits heavily behind my eyes.
The invitations should never have been sent;
this holiday table never set.
Such a waste of cranberry sauce.

My mother looks pretty good
for someone who died forty years ago;
her mother, even better.
The old saying is true then:
death does become them.

In fact, I seem more spirit than they;
no amount of moaning or table tapping
pries their attention away from one another.
It is like watching Christmas dinner
from inside an aquarium.

The tree sits behind them,
festooned with sparkling apologies,
draped with silver remorse -
Ignored.

Words left unspoken
carefully wrapped,
jars of gratitude
tied up with ribbon:
unopened.

Our heirloom angel centrepiece
glued and re-glued annually,
has descended
from attic to table.
My late uncle picks it up
for closer examination;
its head falls off.

This was a really bad idea.
A zoom visit with the grandkids
would probably be better.
I will call,
as soon as the internet is back up.

EARLY MORNING STRATFORD

Crisp shadows,
freshly laundered sun,
grand porches patiently waiting,
with evening stories to tell.

Swept path,
painted steps,
blossoming front yard dreams
of sleepy backyard gardeners.

This town
is too damn good to be true,
but it is real
for this morning.

NOAH'S WATCH

Great grandfather's pocket watch sits
stolid in my desk drawer,
silent patriarch amid the adolescent
noise of pens, paper clips and
post-it notes.

He was a farmer and it was called
a turnip watch.
I let it sit
heavy
in my palm, feel its
pull
toward the earth.

The case barely reflects my face,
the silvered finish now a
patina born of
sweat, soil, wind, and time.

I hold its thick crystal to my ear,
hear the steady stream of ticks
dropping over the edge.

LITTLE MONSTERS

Red sky in the morning,
people take warning.

Step on a crack,
break your mother's back;

The ice is already cracking
up north:
can you hear it?

Listen to your
mother,
mother says:
don't touch that,
you'll get sick,
you'll get sick,
wash your hands,
stay away from that kid.
Don't forget how your aunt died;
don't walk on her grave.
or mine.

Listen to your
father,
father says:
there are no monsters here
but just in case
keep the sheet
over your head,
the closet door latched tight,
just in case.

Downstairs,
high on the mantelpiece,
Happy Halloween,
says the skull with the drunken grin,
and remember:
life is only skin deep.

SMALL COMFORT

Air conditioning
whites out the night,
insulates from
barking dogs,
shifting engines,
warring neighbours,
mindless partying.

No crickets,
wind chimes,
rustling leaves,
humming fridges or
groaning house joints,
no trains in the distance

Ears on full volume,
I try to catch
fugitive vibrations,
make the mental tour:
back yard gate
patio doors,
front door
deadbolt; then

drift back upstairs,
touch down slowly,
still tense.

Worries start to dim;
sleep, just over the horizon.

On the stair landing
a floor board creaks;
outside the bedroom door,
distinct:
a stifled cough.

SPRING LIMBO

Wash of green over winter branches,
skin of ice over spring puddle,
substantial, ephemeral,
temporary, eternal
seasonal, skeletal,
all of these,
none of these,
but for the
observer.

Who stays, who leaves,
what wins, what loses,
my bones, the deadest part of me
outlast all my changes,
echo the winter branches.

PERSPECTIVE

In the old optical illusion,
the witch melts away,
the young beauty
in the hat
takes her place:

Oh, what a world! What a world!
Who would have thought
a good little girl like you
could destroy my beautiful wickedness?

In the illusion of the universe,
dark matter is queen,
black velvet arms
embracing
her glowing young children

HALLOWE'EN 2022

I shiver on our drafty doorstep
as princesses,
slashers,
superheroes
drag their flimsy costumes
over wet pavement
toward our porch.

No soldiers can be seen,
the wars still too fresh;
no time
for blood and oil to dry;
no time
to paper over stains,
hang pictures
in pristine uniformity,
preserve the faces of martyrs.

Long after midnight,
pumpkins quenched,
doors locked,
our kids nestled
all snug in their beds.

Candy wrappers rustle,
skirmish with the leaves
through empty streets,
past darkened windows
of the corner store.

Bolt upright in bed,
I hear it clearly,
a sudden staccato rap,
bony knuckled insistence
at our back door.
Listen...listen I say.
We hold our breath;
the wind quiets to whispers:

We are the dead...

SKETCHES

In the milky January fog,
pencil shadings
by an unsteady hand,
a barn, or perhaps a house,
approaches, then
recedes as we pass.

On the shoulder,
charcoal smudges,
Mennonites in a buggy,
someone on a bicycle,
mailbox sentinels,
defined,
undefined,
gone.

If I pulled over,
parked in this emptiness,
would the memories roll by again?
Could I get them to stop a while?

YARD SALE

Boxes, bins, tables
line the driveway, jumbled
ruins of a domestic earthquake

We wait in plastic chairs,
eight o'clock
a quiet Saturday morning.

At some secret signal
they arrive on foot, in
trucks,
vans,
cars,
a wheelchair.

Some chat casually but
gazes still flit and alight,
drift and settle
and drift.

An old woman
arrives from nowhere,
lumbers across the lawn,

circles the tables wordlessly,
squints,
picks up a vase, a toaster, a book,
shoves each back,
disdainful.

Her hand plunges into a liquor box,
emerges clutching
a stuffed tiger,
my daughter's.

She pokes its plumpness with
yellow fingernails,
tests its fur with a
callused thumb.
I watch as
memories rub off,
dust from a moth's wings.

THE WILDERNESS STARES BACK

It's their gawking that really frosts me,
these creatures with their
cameras, paunch, and sunglasses,
more buggers than bugs,
staining my rocks, flattening my grass.

They pilfer my images,
think their puny screens
can contain my light and colours
until they get home.

I could sear their flank steaks
with my lightning,
send them squealing downhill;
or I could blow them off,
fling them screaming from my cliffs.

But why bother?
It would only confer some sort of
posthumous honour:
martyrdom for the cause of stupidity.

They're finally leaving,
heading down through the forest.
The woods are tinder dry right now.
Come to think of it, I'll go down ahead of
    them.
I really need a good smoke.

CONFLICT MEDIATION

Assembled, we dissemble,
fidget,
watch the clock,
watch the door,
feint and parry.

There is no elephant in this room
but there is something else.

It winds its bulk beneath us,
sandpapers the table legs with its rough skin,
abruptly
cracks its tail against the wood,
startles the rhythm of our hearts.

We do not look down.
to meet this lifeless gaze,
these two dark marbles
floating in murky sentiment.

The air begins to turn
red and cloudy;
it thickens and churns.

I look across at you
but can no longer see your face.

THE CRACK THAT LETS THE DARK IN

It is said you can only carry
light into darkness,
not the other way around -
impossible to touch an absence
and yet,

even walking toward a blazing sun,
the drag of my shadow is
deadweight chainmail,
his feet stitched, Peter Pan-like, to mine.

Turning around,
I could give chase,
to an invisible quarry.
or stand still
and see right through
to the ground.

MY FATHER'S SEA

My father has a depression in his skull,
just at the hairline.
Whenever I sat on his lap
I ran my fingers over it and asked him to tell
    the story
again.

When he was five,
a friend beckoned across the street with
free lead for a mechanical pencil.
My father
ran into the path of a bicycle
coasting downhill and
crawled home,
bloody and dazed.

The hollow is more obvious now
yet still covered by unperturbed skin
like the gentle surface of his sea,
undulating,
never raging,
always reaching shore,
always here.

MORNING TRAIN

My head nods in this
static linear space;
poles and graffiti bump by,
passenger voices muted by
hum and shake,
snack cart monologue
the only tie that binds:

sandwiches,
juice
refreshments
you wanna sandwich?
I got tuna
I got egg salad
I got ham and cheese,
that's not a sandwich, that's a bagel.
no we don't have that
a caramilk?
two dollars
coffee too?
six dollars with
the coffee
last call

coffee

tea

pop...

On the platform at union station,
eyes straight ahead:

> *watch your step,*
> *have a nice day,*
> *watch your step,*
> *have a nice day.*

A woman with a cane
totters,
sways off balance
on the stair:

> *watch your step*
> *have a nice day...*

HOMESTEAD

Her barn taken long ago by tornado,
the house mourns
and follows slowly,
gracefully; she has no choice,
but to proceed with dignity.

For who can shrug off the sun's insistence,
or hide from the creeping melt of snow?
What is to be gained
by arguing with a bullying wind?

Fifteen children born under this roof,
eleven raised,
fanning out their descendants
beyond these fields,
A page turned as each walked away.

Now, turkey vultures nest
in the bedrooms above,
and tales are told
of someone watching
from the windows below.
I wonder who it might be.

I trust they have chosen to stay,
to let the shadows of decades
pass over them,
cool in the depth of memory,
safe from the miasma of a feverish world,
sheltered from the glare of heaven.

THIRD KINGDOM

Once imbued with majesty,
pinnacle of the animals
master of the forests
now sits and watches,
chews and listens,
drinks and dozes,
pasty hobbit in a glass hillside.

What curious thoughts
crawl like beetles between his ears,
kick and die in the wax?

What strange parades
pass by his eyes,
melt away like
doughnut glaze?

Risen from sediment,
now in third place:
the minimal kingdom.

ELIZABETH

1855 - 1920

Elizabeth, where are you?
I search for you
among the tattered pages
of Victorian photo albums.
Flakes of black paper,
like brittle autumn leaves,
break away between my fingers.
Labelled ancestors gaze at me
sombre, stoic,
settled patiently.
Everyone is there except you.

Elizabeth, who were you?
Pledged to God at birth,
unwed mother at thirty,
unmarried at death,
never a hearth of your own.
Labelled *domestic*
between the lines of government census;
labelled *harlot*
between the lines of gossip's censure.

Your young charges said you were small and
    stern
but called you *Lizzie*;
perhaps not so stern,
as to rule out love.

Elizabeth, where are you?
A chestnut mare grazes
in patches of sun
by a country graveyard.
You lie next to your upstairs family,
Enfolded in their plot,
entwined in their past.

Elizabeth who are you?
Sunday morning,
in the front hall mirror,
you smooth and pin
your hair for church.
I stand behind you
and look for your reflection.

SAVING DAYLIGHT

Daylight saving time -
to keep or not to keep -
isn't the real question here.

Instead, I ask:
is there a way to save daylight,
a mason jar
to preserve
the virgin light of childhood,
that pure, undiluted vision
we have, then gradually lose
as scales grow over our eyes?

What bottle can contain
the sun-salted gleaming swells
of ocean eddies and flows;
what vessel, the hot white light
of beach sand,
or the rhythmic coloured shards
of risings and settings;
time breathing in,
breathing out?

How would we freeze-dry
autumn leaves
spotlit
against dark pulsing skies
or the scintillating ermine
of first snowfall
in the evergreen air
of Christmas yet to come?

OUTSIDE

On the street, parked cars
shrouded,
porch lights dormant;
houses bathed in silver silence,
roofs moonlit,
angles softened
with snow.

A spectre of smoke
suspended
over each chimney
to trap errant thoughts.

All arguments interred,
schedules paralyzed;
everyone together now,
dreaming
separate dreams,
yet drifting
under the same quilt.

I stand alone
with my jagged thoughts
and ache
for this gentle communion,
feel the creeping
vertigo of
aloneness,
turn and stride quickly toward home.

My footsteps crack the frozen crust.

MIRROR DREAM

The person in the mirror is not who you are,
Or how you were,
not even who you think you might be
or could have been.

A thin, brittle shadow
of sugar glass
between you and this world -
such easy prey
for frowning brows,
narrowed eyes,
creeping rumours in dirty corners
of coffee shops and laundromats.

So you stand
in a waking dream,
facing your personal
someone else,
avoiding his eyes,
resistant,
resolute,
afraid to turn around.

EKPHRASTIC ELEGY

From the very beginning,
my artistic career
was a tortuous path.
Even my stickmen had deformities,
a bent leg here,
a bizarrely angled arm there,
strange toothless little smiles,
giant claws for toes.

My uncle, who studied
child psychology, said:
isn't that interesting,
all his pictures slope to the left;
he was right,
my stickmen walked downhill;
my dogs walked downhill -
even my ducks,
which for some reason
looked like baby raptors.

So I tried to keep it simple:
ghosts in a snowbank,
black cats in a coal bin

but I forgot the eyes.
My teacher
had a good suggestion though:
why don't you just use black construction
    paper
instead of wasting all that crayon?
She was right too,
subtlety of colour was a challenge.
The little girl next to me
had another good suggestion:
you should try to stay inside the lines.

Once I drew an ancient warrior;
actually, I copied the kid across the aisle.
I thought the drawing was pretty good
but now I realize his breasts weren't quite
    right.
My mother stifled a laugh when she saw it.
I asked her why and she just said:
oh, nothing.

When I reached grade eight
I studied under a master:
our principal held the arts in high esteem;
if you were any good,
she'd let you paint Disney characters
on the windows at Christmastime.
While I drew, she watched over my shoulder:

oh my, you'll never be an artist will you?
It was the most sympathetic thing
anyone ever said to me about my art.

These days I leave the artwork
up to my three year old grandson;
already he surpasses me
with a brilliant mix
of colour and abstract abandon.
The torch is passed;
I go to my grave, content.

LOVE

No sooner born in a cold back room, than
love had died,
more likely was
Swept out and lost
On cleaning day.

For now at dusk as I lie with you,
I hear it cry,
Or think I do,
Somewhere outside,
Somehow alive,

And as I hold this faintest trace,
Sift auburn hair,
wed breath like lace,
twin fireflies,
my quiet prize.

WAITING ROOM

The sign says I must sit in the brown section.
There are no magazines in the brown section
or the grey section for that matter,
just a box of Kleenex ® and
a bottle of hand sanitizer.
This does not bode well.

I sanitize my hands.

Another sign says take a ticket
so take one.
I study it for a while.
It says number ninety-two.
It also says Turn-O-Matic ®

There is a digital clock on the wall –
a special one that counts off seconds,
not just minutes

...35, 36, 37, 38...

A huge picture of a field of wheat

hangs on the other wall.
I imagine I am a mouse
winding my way
through the giant stalks.
Then I imagine a hawk...

...04, 05, 06, 07, 08, 09...

I sanitize my hands again.

There is a television over in the grey section;.
when no one is watching,
I moonwalk to the other side.
On screen is a continuous loop
of starving children.
I slink back to the brown side.

Now I feel like crying.

...56, 57, 58, 59, 00, 01, 02...

I look at my ticket again:;
it still says
ninety-two
and Turnomatic ®

I count the chairs in the brown section,

36
if you must know,
all brown,
as you might expect,
all the same size
except for one -
big enough for two children
or one ample-bottomed adult.
It doesn't look big enough to nap in
but I try,
head against one chrome armrest,
legs jammed
under the other.

...12, 13, 14, 15, 16, 17...

Now I am stuck but
I don't care;
I am somehow relaxed
for reasons
unknown to science;
perhaps it's the instinctive
submission
of the doomed animal.

I may even be able to sleep.

56, 57, 58, 59...

Number 92 please?

HELLO!....
NUMBER 92 !?

PICTURE WINDOW

Arms filled with firewood,
he crosses the backyard drifts;
night snow numbs his legs.

He pauses to study his family
framed in the warmly lit window.

Father on the couch,
brow furrowed,
mind still at work.

Mother gazes into middle distance
at some other past.

His little brother, an only child,
slumps with ponderous emptiness
as he plays on the floor.

Love is there, he thinks,
but oh such a careless love it is.

WRAPPED UP

I wear my age like a hooded cloak,
each minute woven into the wool,
threadbare memories,
patched in
odd places.

But when the wind blows,
snaps
the hem at my legs,
tugs
to unhood me,
I only pull it tighter 'round,
savour its silken lining,
quicken
at the thought of home.

HEAT IN THE PIPES

In winter, blood runs ancient and thick
through its veins,
rusty plasma
bubbles and clicks around our family,
shrouds us in
shadows of tenants past.

If we held a séance
we would not lack sound effects,

If there should be an aneurysm
undiagnosed,
if a hemorrhage should
stain and soften these walls
undetected in the night,
would the house die;
would its soul
puddle
on the floor,
drip slowly through the cracks?
What then of our lives?

HOME ALONE

I wonder what it would be like to stay at
    home,
to live in my family home forever;
there are some folks who apparently do this
long after their parents are interred
in a plastic photo frame.

I can imagine playing a ghost,
haunting my own house,
reading my comics, top of stack to bottom
and back again,
playing the same records over and over
until the grooves know their own lyrics;
living on spam and kraft dinner with ketchup,
captain crunch and twinkies for dessert

until the wrecking ball breaks the spell.

What happens then?
What then, knowing my past
has really passed
and everyone I know has
died or gone away?

School bullies will laugh when they read
    the news
if they remember me at all.

The dust on the windowsill is like
snow,
so thick it sticks to my fingers;
I try not to touch
this perfect surface.

I wear my age like a hooded cloak,
each minute stitched carefully into the lining
by someone else.
So I need not worry,
need not
apologize,
not ever,
no, never.

WALK LIKE A DOG

Among the peasants on the windswept steppes of Lower Translogovia, there is an ancient legend: It is said that if you follow carefully in the footprints of a wolf, you will be imbued with the speed of the wolf, the senses of the wolf, the very spirit of the wolf....

    As I walk across the windswept heights
    of Upper Queens Park,
    I spot large paw prints in the fresh snow,
    Mastiff, Great Dane,
    hard to say.
    I am reminded of the Translogovian myth,
    and am moved to scoff at those primitives:
    Ha! I say loudly,
    and a startled squirrel
    claws its way frantically
    up the nearest tree.

    Then it comes to me:
    What better way
    to disrespect someone's beliefs

than to disprove them?
No wolf prints handy, so these will have to do.
I place one boot carefully in the first paw
    print,
then the next, then the next...

Two legs adapting to a four-legged walk
is awkward at first
but soon I am into the rhythm.
A jogger stops in mid-stride and watches.
I don't care; I'm starting to like this.
It feels like dancing.

Picking up speed,
the wind rippling through my ~~fur~~ hair,
I run across the lawn and follow the
prints onto Parkview Drive,
thank God
no one ever clears their sidewalks.

Then my peripheral eye
spies something:
something yellow and red,
and I am consumed
by a burning primal urge.

I halt abruptly at the fire hydrant
and start circling,

circling,
circling...
What to do?
If I succumb,
if I drop to my knees
and try to lift my leg,
it will finish off my lower back for good.
I am also dimly aware
that people are beginning
to gather around me.

What do dogs do to distract themselves?
Suddenly the answer comes to me:
Stop, drop, and roll.
With a grunt, I pull away
from the hydrantic magnet,
lope
into the nearest yard,
throw myself
down on the snow
and begin to roll and thrash about.

There is now a small crowd
gathered on the sidewalk,
socially distancing from me.
That is so thoughtful.
I love them!
This all feels so good

that I growl in delight -
I can't help myself.

Soon a woman appears
on her front porch,
throws something
onto the snow in front of me.
I seize the soup bone in my teeth
and try to thank her
but it comes out as:
"Aarf aroo".

I smell cigarette smoke and beer
from three porches up,
and fresh popcorn;
someone is selling to the audience
lined up in their cars along the street;
I don't really care.

But then the flashing red lights,
the piercing wail, agony to my ears;
I bare my teeth:
oh no you don't!
Damned if you'll take this away from me...

THE LITTLE KING

Always at the same table,
next to the canadian maples and honey
    crullers,
crowned with a stained baseball cap,
robed in a faded plaid shirt
one size too large
hanging open,
a sheen of greasy stubble
speckling
his royal visage.

He holds daily court with his chosen few.
They also wear baseball hats
out of respect.

Dribbles
of coffee on his chin,
he pronounces on the workings of the world:
the mayor - links with the Guelph mafia,
the prime minister - on the take,
Schwarzenegger - a transvestite.

He knows this for certain
from a reliable source.

On hot summer days
he promenades shirtless,
down the avenue,
magnificent white belly
preceding him
like the prow of a grand sailboat.

Behind him, his little girl,
legs pumping, out of breath.

Hurry up he commands,
I haven't got all day.

EVERY NIGHT

The rain has purchased
no relief
on this dead-end street;
voided humidity languishes in
puddles; sweat
exudes from factory pores,
the dogged smell of
worker lives lived
at the bottom of the sea.

And every night
the sun goes down in
flames.

CHATEAU DE CHAMBORD

At times my mongrel mind worries away at
    itself,
chewing on its own tail
then licking the hairs
from between its teeth.

Like a mobius loop,
It competes with itself
for redundancy.

...if I am proud of myself but ashamed of my pride should I be
ashamed of myself if it is better to give than receive am I then
selfish in my insistent generosity when I listen with reply l as
my sole purpose do I really hear you when my offered advice is
unsolicited, is it also unwelcome worse yet unheeded....

Meanwhile,
over at Chateau de Chambord,
the double helix staircase
continues to confuse visitors.
Was it designed by

da Vinci,
da Cortona
or da both of them?

If there were two of me,
I could bypass myself
ascending or descending
without ever seeing
who I was.

CHRISTMAS OF A CERTAIN YEAR

In the end,
wrappings crumpled in a glad bag,
sullen pools of grease sit in the pan,
decorations hang like regrets over the door.

Last grudges
stuck in the carpet
like pine needles;
with any luck
they will work themselves out
by next year.

Next year
we will plan, shop, bake, decorate,
    wrap things up tighter,
much tighter,
so nothing
we haven't planned for
comes down the chimney.

Next year for sure.

This evening everyone talks,
no one listens
or hears the
    back door close.

In the white lawn chair in
the whiteness I watch
large flakes, like my mother's
laundry soap,
gather on my coat sleeves
    faster and thicker.

I wait for them to blanket me;
my father said it snowed like this
the night I was born.

WRAPPINGS

Gifts are wrapped first in boxes,
then in paper
and finally enfolded
in the hands of the giver.

Many are enveloped
in cold silver hands,
folded and perfect,
sharply defined,
seeking to oblige,
or to banish guilt.

Some come wrapped
between the hands of age,
thin like parchment,
dry and veined,
whispering accrued wisdom and love
into the ears of your skin.

Others are cupped
in the chubby hands of children,
messy and eager,

seeking only to surprise
and to warm themselves
in your joy.

DIE RATZE

Translation:
ratz = rat
ratze = plural of rat
ratzen = to nap
(difficult with ratze in the haus)

They say every animal
is God's creature,
has a role in nature's plan,
snaps into the ecosystem
like a Lego® brick,
so to speak.

Ratze seem a bit different,
little ratzi stormtroopers,
gliding through the dark
on dirty little ratzi feet
slick with invisible God knows what.

If a ratz catches his head in a ratz trap
his colleagues may rescue him
by surgically removing his body,
leaving its hairy little skull
staring from the trap,
with its beady little ratz eyes.

Ratze formed a commune
under our chicken coop last year.
I don't believe any of them were married,
at least not to each other.

Apparently ratze send out reconnaissance
        scouts.
One night when I stood very still,
two of them tiptoed as far as my boots
then moonwalked back into the wall.

Much to our dismay,
we soon found we had become
perpetrators of ratzocide -
shootings, drownings, trappings, poisonings -
nothing seemed beneath us
as we disturbed the order of nature.

Axe to ratz combat
was the most difficult,
morally speaking.
I don't know whether a rat can beseech,
but I swear this one did.
As I swung, I had to close my eyes
and nearly severed my foot.

YOU CAN HEAR THE ROBINS ON MAIN STREET

Like a Sunday afternoon in 1957
exquisite blandness
sun-soaks the streets,
the storefronts like books unopened,
the streets grand and open trails
to a midsummer night's countryside.

Abnormal creature am I,
some sort of mutation, I fear,
not to miss the buzz and flight,
the endless cycles of
hiving and stinging
looping and spiralling our days into
weeks,
months,
all the years
preceding the fall.

A stranger's singular smile in passing
takes root in my mind,
spreads and blossoms.
We can both hear the robins on Main Street.

FOR MY NEW GRANDSON

Over the depths of day
we float,
your hair a downy crown,
your soft life so quiet upon my chest,
but for each small reassuring sigh.

We share the brushstrokes of new dreams.

Downriver through uncertain night,
droplets of minutes,
ripples of hours
the tides of passing days.

When we drift apart,
find me again on the banks,
place your ear next to my heart
and remember who I was.

FANTASIES

At each sunset,
the wind speaks,
blows my fantasies about
like ashes after a forest fire.

The flawless field,
the lush forest
are pixilated in retrospect,
blurred, imperfect,
imbued with smoke and regret.

At each sunrise,
my fevered dreams,
full of dread and hesitation,
pop like bubbles,
melt into clear sky;
harping wraiths,
sharp-toothed detractors
grapple and grope,
find no purchase,
and tumble over the precipice.

My prayers are for
healing and unity,
a reconciliation of branches
in the bole of the tree,
upright and heedless
in the face of the
bellicose midday sun.

CLOTHESLINE

Wrists pinned and stretched,
buoyed yet captive within the
wind,
transfixed as seasons
tumble over the
horizon.

Inside the roar,
empty arms flap and whip,
snap silently at each
shrinking sunset.

Starched and taut that no
sigh may crack the fabric of this life,
spun and dried that no
tear may stain this
creased and collared crime.

STEPPING BACK

No man ever steps in the same river twice,
for it's not the same river and he's not the
same man.

There are times I must respectfully
disagree with Heraclitus;
when I open a stick of chewing gum or
smell a cigar freshly lit,
I am immediately sitting next to my father
in a patch of sunlight
on our side steps,
torn down decades ago.

And opening any cedar chest,
these blankets must surely be my mother's.

Even the musty vapour of exhaust
on a clear February day
sits me back behind myself
where I was passenger, not driver.

Yet deep in dreams where I should
roam free in my home town,

stubborn shadows blur the
faces of passersby.

I stare through the window of a closed store
on main street and know
Thomas Wolfe was right.

THE GOOD LIFE

life's not so easy in this neighbourhood
fred always thinks we got it so good that's
because he doesn't have to live here

people are movin' in
who could well afford
to stay where they belong.
damn hard luck stories don't
fool me
where's the remote
who keeps moving the remote

I told our MP but he didn't listen and
it's too late now look at the colour they
painted their house
disgusting
why do you always buy t-bone you know
I like ribeye
where the hell is the remote

have you been to the mall lately, seen all
    those lazy
assholes the mall used to be safe now there's
    always
somebody in your face with their
hand in your pocket
put them to work make them
pay back their fucking welfare
damn this candy always
sticks to my teeth
why don't you buy chips
once in a while
where did you put the remote I said

air conditioning wasn't working in the
lexus again
don't we have any beer left
can't I get a drink in my own house
didn't you wash my shirt yet
fucking candy
where's the remote
where the fuck are you going?

DEAD CENTRE

Rain remnants
trickle off leaves onto
new mown lawn
startled green.

Dead centre,
yellow leaf
asterisk that says
you are here.

TENTATIVE GRASP

In the quantum brew,
beneath the substrata of life,
causes without cause,
appearances without origin,
connections without touch,
objects without shape.

At the core
of my fragile flesh,
of my still undissected
beating heart,
blindness to colour,
tone deafness
to competing rhythms,
hot and cold
meld together,
cupped boundary of
yin and yang
no more tangible
than angles of longitude.

Now before me ranges
delirious veracity,
delicious latitude,
rolling vista of the ages,
panorama of the cosmos.

MCEERIE'S CURIOSITY SHOP

Perhaps it was the pig skull
on the piano
or the wild boar head
on the wall
that got my attention.

Maybe it was the mummified carp,
with gaping mouth
or the white rabbit head
grafted
onto the taxidermied snowy owl
that occasioned
a certain frisson.

Possibly it was
the miniature
coin operated
electric chair,
complete with fried felon,
or the change purses crafted
from genuine cane toads
that moved me.

Then again -
it could have been the mannequin
in the straitjacket,
although straitjackets
are not unique
and are readily available online
in a variety of styles and colours.

For a moment,
this sideshow,
this oasis of weirdness,
made me forget myself.
All is not lost;
I have hope now.
I am definitely coming back to this place.

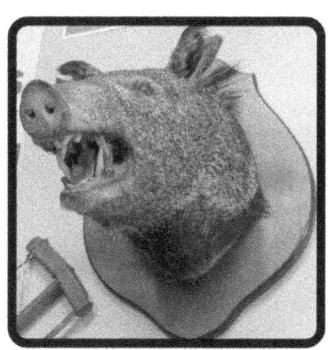

MILES AWAY AT HOME

In a backyard sky without borders,
I can feel, not hear
the distant screams of children;
picture, not see them.
My web of lilac and birdsong
almost protects me.

In a room without definition,
the television casts a net
of pixels and particles,
of bake shows and bargains,
snags my fears before they snap,
or most of them.
Shivers of colour
dart across my couch.

In dreams without escape,
the boil is lanced,
lava flows hungrily,
eager to choke my valley,
to fill the void
with darkness.

JACK AND EDNA ON THE TRAIN

Jack sways
against the rhythm of the tracks,
half sits,
half falls
into a seat;
takes off his bucket hat,
mops his brow,
breathing hard.

Edna trots
behind with the Samsonite,
takes a seat across the aisle.
Jack needs lots of room.

You ok?

Jack confirms
in a submerged baritone,
waves a knobby hand
to swat away her worry.

Edna's bird-like hand
shoots across the aisle:

Here, use your chapstick.

Grunt.

Breath mints soon follow:

Don't forget these.

Mumble.

Edna soon occupies herself with
Christmas shopping; asks the
service representative about every item in the
Official Via Souvenir Case:
coffee mugs, playing cards,
stuffed bears, decorative spoons;
each sports the Via emblem;
each is presented to Jack for his input.

In Georgetown,
Edna watches passengers disembark.
As the train starts moving again she says:

They sure don't give you much time to get off,
    do they?

At Union Station,
Jack is on his feet,
before the train fully stops;
    suitcase in hand,
he lumbers down
the narrow steps
to the platform.
Edna is nowhere to be seen.

Where the hell is she?

Edna returns from the washroom,
looks panicked for a second, then
purses her lips and says:

Probably took the wrong exit;
that man is so impatient.

ZONED IN

Intemperate, intransigent,
of this we were warned,
in this now certain:
the winds at cross purposes,
bears stalking south,
wasps streaking north
thunder in winter,
water like a mad dog
licking at our toes
then thirsty for our throats;
we sweat and water our lawns.

And the snow grows deeper
in our cold, cold hearts.

In illusion, one planet;
in reality worlds collide;
in future, in situ,
our plastic grave goods blown
free of sand,
naked and insolent.

Incalcitrant,
we dream of seasons,
of beaches,
of Christmas,
of strange lost animals.

And the snow grows deeper
in our cold, cold hearts.

OCEANIA

(OR PISSING INTO THE WIND)

I have to hand it to the Polynesians,
sailing into the wind like that,
tacking and shunting
zigzagging
until they ran out of islands,
or patience.

Then they said:
that's it, mates
and let the trade winds
blow them back home;
chugged back
some coconut wine,
smoked
a few big fat Samoan cigars
to pass the time.

I doubt I have any Polynesian DNA;
the gods at ancestry.ca thought I was
one hundred thousandth Micronesian
but later changed their minds,
revoked my genealogy,

and yet,

I am forever sailing upwind,
sidestepping, feinting
ducking, dodging;
facefuls of ocean water
sting my eyes,
rime my lips with salt.

Maybe it's time
to lie back in my outrigger,
let my past fold back into itself
like origami,
and drift
through deep blue
into aquamarine.

On the beach,
someone else's parents
wait for me
but I embrace them,
follow them home,
watch the sunset with them;

Last one in turns out the lights.

APRIL

The winter months,
buttoned up,
buttoned down
like bankers,
march home from work,
all dark suited,
heavy booted
rime of worry
on their brows
flurry of footsteps then

distance,
silence
spiraling into
a deep bright
singularity:

this moment we named April.

OUTLOOK

If I were to say to you,
as we barbecue our steaks,
that the pit of hell is below us
and volcanic snow falls among us
silent and unseen,
would you shake your head
and crack another beer?
If I point out,
on this cold day of mourning,
that your mother now dances
in her youth
in meadows of buttercups
and Queen Anne's lace,
the warm wind all around her,
would you turn away with bitter tears?
But tonight on this moonlit hill,
can you see
the web of cosmos
spinning itself
into gossamer roads,
branching into virgin paths untried,
but as broken as each sunrise?

Can you consider
this moment alone,
without slipping?

STILL LIFE WITH SQUIRREL

Oh thou sad creature!
This fine morning I came upon thee
fallen by the wayside,
crouched in mid-scramble,
thy jet eyes glistening in sunlight,
thy bushy tail floofing in the breeze.

Oh that I had known thee in life!
I would have given thee counsel
against the scurry and toil
of thy rodent lifestyle,
thy ceaseless climbing,
endless deposits
in mine grass,
endless withdrawals
from mine garden
and from mine bird feeder.

Oh, would that thou had made peace
and did share merriment
with thy neighbours;
that thy tiny life had been free
of chatter and skirmish;

that thou had paused
and reflected
and listened
and looked both ways...

Oh pathetic little one!
Anon thou art paused
in eternity,
thy brief life a study
in taxidermy.

TIME'S DAUGHTER

Truth is the daughter of time, not authority.
- Sir Francis Bacon

I can still make out her filmy gown.
It floats, ripples
beneath my carefully cast
nets of routine.
Will she surface
before transparency
clouds?

I slice each month
cleanly,
evenly,
before it leaves the pan,
before it can cool.

Outside the kitchen door,
she waits;
her winter children
will soon nibble at my mind;
her rough tongue

will explore my heart,
eager but patient.

IN A DIFFERENT LIGHT

On midlife tongue sits the
soursweet taste of seasons,
raw rhubarb dipped in sugar,
rhythm of the lawn swing in June,
apple butter and cottage cheese in
flat grey light of
November mornings.

I should have savoured the boredom,
the delicious loneliness.

Staring up through the trees,
on the cusp of now and then,
branches vein the
swollen clouds above;
storm front fingertips
rustle cool and soft in the elms.

The crows are silent at the
end of the lane.

THE BEST WOMEN

I've always been drawn to intelligent women,
     perhaps
another example of opposites attracting but
I would highly recommend their company any
     time.
Encyclopaedias and dictionaries are no longer
required in your home so you will have
extra shelf space for novels and comic books.
You will discover that your brain can coast for
     lengthy intervals;
there is no need for struggling
to grasp the obvious.

THE ATTIC IN WINTER

I don't mind the attic,
still and settled,
the wind's exhalation
all I can hear of the fretful world.

As a child I was boosted through
the hatch
to help rescue Christmas,
lower her
back into the warmth
for the brief now
that was then.

Last week I tried to clean up,
but couldn't;
opening the wrong box
might allow sunshine to
escape,
evaporate
through the roof vents
or memories to
melt
in the harshness of my flashlight.

Better to sit in
sad, sweet contemplation
of the brief then
that is now.

THE CARELESSNESS OF HOPE

This is the year,
these are the days
when even hope is
an unwelcome, chattering visitor,
a careless guest
with dirty hands
who leaves the door ajar
as she departs.

These are the hours,
these are the minutes,
the seconds
when pain is a loyal friend,
present
and honest,
keeping us awake
in its arms.

This is the time of glasses
half full,
half empty;
pick yours up,

smash it in the fireplace,
let the wine evaporate.

BEACH TOWN

A tattered crew,
we mismatched
sailors of tourism
In flip-flops and sunglasses,
cruising down main street through
waves of flotsam and jetsam.
stale fudge, corn dogs,
mood rings, certificates of
beer drinking prowess.

First raindrops fall, release
dusty dampness
into this parade,
a promise to wash us clean,
sweep us back to the
sea whence we came,
perhaps never to start up
again.

BEDTIME STORY

Part One

In the amber pool of my bedside lamp,
my father sits,
storybook open.

Feet propped against the warmth of his leg,
hands clasped behind my head,
eyes closed;
images flash through
corridors of story as I
drift.

We arrive at chapter's precipice:
"suddenly, a dark shape leapt from the
        corner..."
and it is nine o'clock.

I plead, beg, barter:
one more chapter,
two more pages,
one more page,
I must know how it ends.

Part Two

In the darkness
all bets and bargains off,
feet jammed against the footboard,
rough texture of heartbeat against
cold sheets,
slide toward the precipice of
fatal worry.
If I should die before I wake ...

I open my eyes.
I will not go
before the story ends.

AT ODDS

I sometimes reprimand myself
for an ill-chosen word,
a thoughtless comment,
a lost pair of glasses,
some device connected in reverse.

Sometimes I even call myself names.

I do argue back, though.
This is when it starts getting bad.
Words fly back and forth,
words no decent person should have to hear.
words that question
my heritage,
my religion,
even my anatomy.

Worst of all, is when it gets physical.
To hold yourself in a headlock
for any length of time
defines a whole new threshold of pain,
as my chiropractor will tell you;

to thrust your own face into a bowl of
    porridge is
a different level of humiliation,
as my therapist will tell you.

It becomes quite alarming,
particularly when I get a good
stranglehold on my throat.
This is where my mother usually steps in:
boys, boys, stop that now.

Perhaps I only imagine this last part.
My mother is dead,
God rest her soul.

SMALL TOWN EYES

In the dim light of the pub
I can almost believe it was
then,
not now,
almost hear those words:
hey you, c'mere.

Only the cigarette smoke is missing.

My feet seem to be under water;
I move back to my table;
the same eyes stare
in dull assessment;
same eyes narrow
in shallow judgement;
same old eyes
sunken in an older face.

And was that a smirk I saw?

This time I stare back.
I know you;
I know you well.

I could figure out
which car is yours,
you know;
slip outside and drag my key
hard and deep,
rip your nice glossy surface:
such a satisfying sound.

We'll see how cool you are then.

As I turn away
I hear a voice,
almost a whisper:
hey buddy, you ok?

IN SKIES OVER CALGARY

In holding pattern
our thin metal craft shudders,
an eggshell apt to split and
spill us like oatmeal from the
stirred,
gut-swollen clouds.

Beyond the window glass,
dark primordial vapour
evokes Nemo's Nautilus,
imperial hull gaping,
dynamos leaking orange
lightning;
with each visceral
crack our hearts
jumpstart anew:
sparks over the bonfire.

AT THE END OF OUR TIME

At the end of our time,
at the very bottom
of the physical mystery,
we are of the same ether;
the breath of Hitler
mingles in the atmosphere
with the breath of Gandhi;
molecules shed
from our discarded bodies,
mix in the earth's mantle
with the bones of dinosaurs
and mice.

And what of our memories,
of sunsets seen,
of the love we've felt?
What substance did they possess?
Were they only there
because we were there
to perceive them?

At the end of time,
at the very edge

of mind,
there is a light,
it is said, we should follow
where ancient beauty
waits with depthless love,
where all we have been,
all we have become and will be,
is one with an infinite concourse
and the past evaporates
like mist from a mirror.

AUGUST THE TRAITOR

August transitory,
traitor August ,
imminence, not eminence;
corn leaves
conspire, click sabers,
assemble soft rustles
to conceal stealthy autumn:
now steady in the stalk,
soon to be stumps
beneath turncoat skies
under winter's blundering march.

HERE AND THEN

My brother and I remember it differently,
that Christmas when she died,
each memory of each conversation,
fragile and bipolar,
painful or peaceful.
We reimagine the past,
just as surely
as we imagine the future.

I do know
what she said to me near the end:
they shoot horses, don't they.

I also know this:
unbridled guilt is useless,
but dangerous,
a kick to the gut
by a panicked gelding.

I seek to dwell
solely in this moment,
which instantly slips away.
The leaves on our oak

begin to yellow and curl
toward spring
when saplings will
struggle upward,
breaking ground,
gasping for first breath,
stretching toward first winter.

A final certainty:
everyone leaves
sooner or later.

SECOND SLEEP

The morning light bleeds
through sticky eyelids
and I feel
what a contortionist must feel,
taste
what I think
gunpowder
must taste like.

I turn over,
find myself sitting
on a hill
with my back
to the churchyard;
my headstone is behind me;
impossible
but quite acceptable,
perfectly fair.

Breezy sun
below
in an empty valley;
no creature stirs or twitches;

only the grass ripples,
dead but alive
like a sleeping dog
chasing a dream

I should return
to whatever place I was in before
but I have no desire;
my resistance is lax.
Effort should be avoided.
Effort contorts.
When does effort
become redundant?

AFTER THE FALL

There is a certain comfort
in clearing away the snowfall,
sculpting the aftermath
into geometric figures,
straight edge,
level surface,
a mortal symmetry
with deep channels leading
somewhere.

Beneath, something with sharp teeth
twitches in its sleep;
bulbs and roots pulse
with chaotic potential.

Above, the dark and heedless clouds.

SCRATCHBOARD

To find the light
first scratch away the darkness ,
funnel away the dark wind,
the black snow;
attack the opaque.

I am my own mortician,
scraping out my shell,
layer upon layer
of calcified pain.
Like plaster of paris I am
dry
as the floor of a miser's heart,
empty
as spent wrapping paper
on boxing day.

Below,
a murmur of light,
a whisper of rhyme;
I strain for notes
just beneath hearing,
glimpse a glow

of yellow bricks,
tips of emerald spires.

Second star to the right
and straight on 'til morning.

CROW

Each morning
a murder in the tree
down our lane;
blurs of black,
echoing caws
ripping the mist.

Underneath,
an insidious subtext
of communal gossip,
click, rattle, croak and squawk;
whether meant to give comfort
or provoke envy,
it all seems the same.

One tree over,
hidden from the voyeur sun,

a loner
sits,
a figurine
perched
within the leaves' clinging gloom.

Whether to
to take flight
and seek the indifferent
company of thieves,
or remain
an exclamation mark
with no reference point...

He tilts his head,
then spreads his wings.

AFTERWORD

PRAISE FOR WHAT FOLLOWS

Cast adrift in this sea of life,
no friends,
no comrades
but two -
buttock left and buttock right -
without them we'd be ...
askew.

They follow us daily
like faithful dogs,
precede us at night to our beds;
in times of nuclear warfare
provide shelter for our heads.

They absorb the shock of McDonald's seats,
and the boots of well meaning friends,
protect our bones from the winter cold,
and the place our digestive tract ends.

No one's without them,
Jolie nor Pitt,
Einstein, his son, nor his bride.
Donald the Trump even has a set
Which is better left undescribed.

So raise a glass to the sky, my friend;
be sure to do it soon;
drink to the health of what's behind
and bask in the glow of your moon.

ABOUT THE AUTHOR

Mark Hertzberger is a member of The League of Canadian Poets, The Ontario Poetry Society, Poetry Stratford and the Huron Poetry Collective. His first book of poetry, *Fog & Mirrors,* was published in 2019. Among other publications, his poems have also appeared in *Denouement,* published by Beliveau Books and *The Leaf,* published by Brucedale Press.

Mark took first place in the 2008 Poetry Stratford Open Mike Contest and 3rd prize in the K. Valerie Connor 2024 Poetry Contest. He has read his poetry on CJCS Radio and at *Culture Days* festivals in Stratford, Ontario. Mark resides in Stratford with his wife, novelist Yvonne Hertzberger.

PREVIOUS PUBLICATION CREDITS

- *Between,* first published in *The Leaf* by Brucedale Press, 2021
- *Homestead,* first published in *Denouement* by Beliveau Books, 2021
- *Clothesline,* first published in *Writers Undercover: Tenth Anniversary Issue* by The Cambridge Writers Collective, 2004
- *Dawn of Humanity* first published in *The Language of Dew and Sunsets* by The Huron Poetry Collective
- *You Can Hear the Robins on Main Street,* first published in *Fresh Voices* by The League of Canadian Poets
- *Ekphrastic Elegy,* first published in *Verse Afire,* by The Ontario Society of Poets, January 2024

www.ingramcontent.com/pod-product-compliance
Lightning Source LLC
LaVergne TN
LVHW090619260325
806752LV00004B/201